Training the Quarter Horse Jumper

Training the Quarter Horse Jumper

H. Patricia Levings

South Brunswick and New York: A. S. Barnes and Company
London: Thomas Yoseloff Ltd

A. S. Barnes and Co., Inc.
Cranbury, New Jersey 08512

Thomas Yoseloff Ltd
18 Charing Cross Road
London, W.C. 2, England

frontispiece

H. Patricia Levings, mounted on her favorite hunter, Jubilee Red. Jubilee Red, is not only an adept hunter, but is equally proficient under western tack, reining, working cattle, working a rope, working colts, or—just plain pleasure riding.

6679
Printed in the United States of America

**To Pamela Del Rayo,
for her faithful loyalty.**

Acknowledgment

I would like to extend a special Thank You, to Mr. Dick Schinzing, of the M-S Photo Studio for his conscientious help and cooperation in obtaining the photographs appearing in this volume.

Preface

The American Quarter Horse has without a doubt contributed more to the advancement of western horsemanship, and bestowed more general enjoyment on a greater number of our American population than any other horse in America today.

He is owned, ridden, shown, rodeoed, raced, and just plain enjoyed by the man on a budget as well as the millionaire.

There have been, and in fact still are, a few Quarter Horses competing in English classes as well as their own western classes. But as a whole this venture into the realm of the hunter and jumper is comparatively very new. This book was written with the average Quarter Horse owner — who has ridden his Quarter Horse under western tack all his life and now wishes to convert his horse into a dual purpose Western-English mount — in mind.

The schooling of the colt is bypassed, and we start with the present well broke average mature Quarter Horse. Perhaps he has been shown before, or it could be that he has never been in a show ring; but his main purpose has been to bring relaxation and enjoyment to his present owner.

I hope this book will be of help in showing the western rider the way to a successful relationship with his Quarter Horse in this venture and to develop a better understanding of this phase of horsemanship. I hope it will contribute to the advancement of the Quarter Horse as well as serving as an incentive for better and more challenging hunter and jumper courses; for this is the only way, with the aid of interested and enthusiastic owners, that the American Quarter Horse can really progress in this new area.

I hope this book will help the reader in developing his horse into a well conditioned stable animal. To develop techniques that will help achieve a better relationship and harmony between himself and the horse, and for the western rider who admires the jumper — but does not care to actively participate in the activity — a better understanding and appreciation of this school of horsemanship.

H. Patricia Levings
Fine Acres Farm

Contents

Training the Quarter Horse Jumper

I

From Western to English

There are many people who are glad to see the American Quarter Horse Association enter and approve a jumping class in its official rule book. Hunter enthusiasts are equally delighted with the American Quarter Horse Association's decision at its 1966 convention to place a working hunter class among its point-earning events. This will become effective with the 1967 show season.

The American Quarter Horse — with his powerful muscles, even temperment, and versatility — will make a ready candidate for these classes.

Let us assume you have a good Quarter Horse. He is well broke, and you have perhaps been showing him in pleasure classes, or maybe, just riding him for exercise and relaxation. You have always enjoyed watching the hunter and jumper classes at the open shows and secretly wished you too could share in the thrills. Now the time has come when you can participate in this phase of horsemanship.

The first step in successfully schooling the quarter horse jumper is the correct equipment. It is preferable to start your prospective Quarter Horse jumper or hunter in a good hunting bridle with large flat ring hunting snaffle bit. This is a piece of tack well worth the expense as it can always be called into use. However there are two other types of bridles and methods of bitting used on hunters and jumpers. These are the pelham bit and bridle and the full bridle.

The pelham bridle is equipped with a pelham bit to which are attached the

The hunt bridle with the large flat ringed snaffle bit. A valuable piece of tack in any stable.

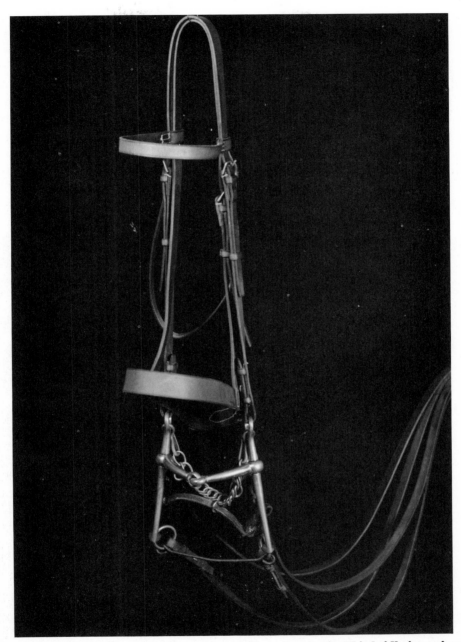

The pelham bridle. A combination of the snaffle and curb bit. This bridle is equipped with the jointed mouth pelham bit.

four reins. One set is attached to the large rings at the mouth, while the second set is attached to the rings of the curb. The wider rein is the snaffle rein, while the narrower rein is the curb rein. This bit is actually a combination of the snaffle and curb bit. However the curb and snaffle action cannot be employed simultaneously as in the case of the full bridle.

The full bridle is as the name implies, a full bridle complete with curb and bradoon, or snaffle bits. Here the wider set of reins are attached to the bradoon and the narrower to the curb bit. Great care must be exercised when fitting this bridle to the horse as he is carrying two separate bits in his mouth. The bradoon should rest in the horse's mouth in approximately the same position as an ordinary snaffle, and the curb should be adjusted so it rests below this. If the horse should be accidently subjected to a hard accidental jerk on the curb

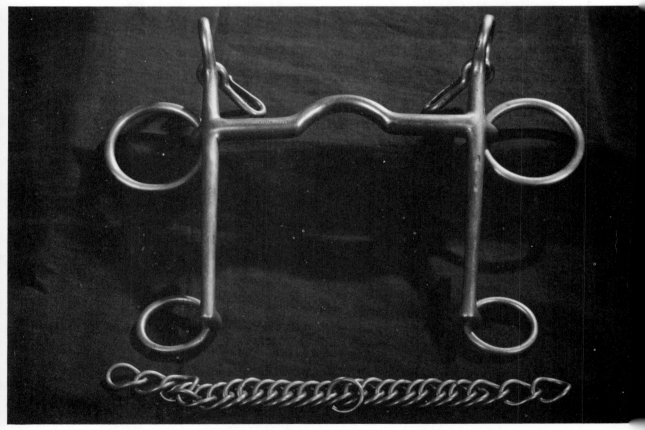

Another style pelham bit with the regular port mouth piece. This standard flat English curb chain, which is at least one-half inch wide is permissable for the A.Q.H.A. jumping and working hunter classes.

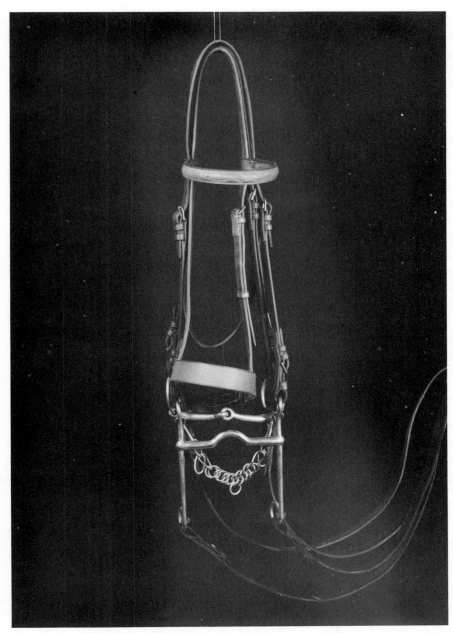

The double or full bridle complete with the bradoon, or snaffle bit and the curb bit.
The two bits permit a rider to use each bit separately or simultaneously as required.

and the bradoon were found to be resting on top of the curb bit, the roof of the mouth could be severely damaged. The same applies if the bradoon should become lodged under the curb. Here the tongue may be severely lacerated. One must always take into consideration that proper adjustment and bitting of the individual horse is paramount.

When you are choosing a forward seat jumping saddle, choose one of the models on the market that are made with a wide tree. These were especially designed for the heavier withered flatter backed horse. Many flat saddles are designed for the Thoroughbred type horse and will not fit your Quarter Horse. Check very carefully through your local saddle shops and catalogs before your final purchase. This will eliminate a good deal of grief later on in the way of sore backs, pinched withers, and a growing distaste for the sight of the jumping saddle on the part of your horse.

It is advisable to use a light pad under your saddle during hacking and schooling sessions. If you plan to show your horse without his pad, it is a wise thing to ride him without it just enough to accustom him to the different feel of the saddle.

After using your saddle and bridle always be sure it is cleaned and put on a rack. The least bit of dirt and sweat left on your tack can start to cause an irritation on the horse. Pay special attention to the girth. Most jumping saddles carry a leather girth. Make sure that it is always kept clean and soft. The same good sensible care of your western gear applies to your jumping tack as well.

You now have your saddle and bridle. Proceeding to the stable, you groom your Quarter Horse until he shines like a new dollar. Then introduce him to the new tack, letting him sniff and smell the saddle thoroughly before attempting to place it on his back. Make sure the stirrups are run up the leathers, to prevent them from striking the horse in the ribs when you place the saddle on his back. Then proceed to set the saddle on the horse. At this point you have it on him, and perhaps it appears the flaps of the saddle are entirely too far forward. Check the saddle at the pommel, it should rest forward in approximately the same place as your western saddle does. Drawing the girth up, it should rest in about the same position as a three-quarter-rigged western saddle's cinch. You now have the horse saddled. At first due to the strange feel and position of the forward flaps against his shoulders, your horse may roll his eyes and turn around to blow softly at this strange new saddle. Reassure him and let him be quiet until he has accepted it. Even though he is a well broke horse, this tack is a new experience, and it is essential that it be introduced calmly and quietly.

Now bridle your Quarter Horse with the hunting snaffle bridle. Adjust the headstall so that the bit rests gently in the corners of the mouth without causing folds (too tight) or showing a space between the bit and the corners of the

The forward seat jumping saddle in place on our Quarter Horse. This saddle is being used without a pad or saddle cloth.

mouth (too loose). After the bridle is on and adjusted correctly, it would be well to lead your horse about the stable yard for a few moments.

At this point I am sure you can hardly restrain yourself from leaping into the saddle, shouting "Tally Ho, Pip Pip and Away!" and go galloping off in hot pursuit of an imaginary pack of baying fox hounds. But good sense and patience win out at this point.

Let us assume your horse reins well, and has all but forgotten the direct rein. Here it is advisable to put a pair of long lines on him. These are fastened to the bit and run back through the stirrups, which have been joined to each other by a strap under the horse's belly. If a strap is not available a piece of quarter-inch cotton cord will do very nicely. This will prevent the stirrups from swinging and hitting the animal and will also help to avoid an accidental jerk on his mouth from the lines should he resist and the stirrups fly up; and when driving on the circle it will keep the stirrups close to his side and prevent them striking him when direction is changed.

Jubilee Red models the hunt bridle with snaffle bit properly adjusted. Plain English hunt reins are being used here. Some hunt bridles are equipped with a laced rein. The laced rein is considered a little more secure as the hand has less tendency to slip. However, the laced rein is a matter of individual preference.

The ideal line is the customary extra-long leather line. But perhaps your budget is small and you are not fortunate enough to have a full complement of training equipment in your tack room. If this is the case there are less expensive but nevertheless serviceable materials that can be utilized. One of these is a good grade quarter-inch cotton cord. Snaps can easily be attached to one end while leather stops made from heavy pieces of scrap leather are fitted to the other end. By chance if you are using these long lines on a green colt with a breaking harness, by dint of the leather stops you are less apt to loose him during an anxious moment.

We now pick up the lines and standing to the rear and slightly to one side

Snipper Socks, saddled, bridled, and equipped with the long lines ready to move out. Note quarter-inch cotton cord to hold the stirrups at the horse's side. Also notice the position of the stirrups to insure free and easy manipulation of the long lines. Notice leather stops on the ends of the long lines. These prevent the lines from being pulled through the trainer's hand during an anxious moment.

At first your horse will probably offer some resistance by trying to turn and come towards you. Keep the opposite line low, and just taut enough to prevent him from turning around to you. Notice Snipper's ear attentive to the trainer, also slightly enlarged nostril and all over attitude of inquiry in this new situation. Firm but quiet insistence at this point is essential.

of the animal we urge him on. At this point he may try to turn and come to you; but by keeping the opposite line low, just above the hocks, and just taut enough to prevent him from turning on you, urge him by voice and a light tap on the hips with the training whip to walk out. After a few moments he should get the idea and move out. You may now do a series of large circles, interspersed with just straight line driving and serpentines, back and forth across an area. It is also advisable to practice backing in the long lines. If your horse has had an old problem of backing crooked this little exercise will be of help in correcting this. Every so often it is wise to stop your horse and make him stand in place, quietly and relaxed. Speak kindly to him to let him know he is obeying correctly. A few sessions of ground driving will really pay off when you mount your future Quarter Horse jumper for the first time.

Now let us assume that your Quarter Horse has accepted his new tack with discretion and is guiding well in the long lines. You are now ready to mount.

When you mount your horse for the first time under this tack, after no doubt a good number of years' acquaintance with a stock saddle, you have the tendency to wonder where the saddle has disappeared to. After a few moments' orientation you begin to feel more at home. You are now ready to familiarize yourself with the seat of this saddle and feel the gaits of your horse.

We are concerned with schooling the Quarter Horse as a jumper, so I will not go into a lengthy dissertation on the fundamentals of the forward seat at this time.

Mounted at last and ready to move out! A good deal of time should be spent riding at the walk and trot, learning to hold the correct position in the saddle and suppling the wrists, while learning to maintain a light contact

Poll flexed, body straight, Snipper is relaxing to the new situation and beginning to get the idea of what is expected of him. Notice stirrups remain in the desired position, even though the horse has previously shown a degree of resistance.

Working on the circle, quiet and relaxed. Though one ear is attentive to the trainer, Snipper is looking ahead and moving along on a light contact of the long lines.

with your horse. This will be very important later on. These things should be worked at and practiced diligently so that when the time comes to jump your horse mounted, you will be as ready as he is, both physically and mentally.

Now that you and your horse are getting together on this new venture, it is time to start some simple exercises to supple and condition your horse.

Jumping requires an athletic agility as well as a mental agility. At this stage of schooling, work at suppling the horse, stabilizing his gaits and reaching a stable mental attitude is most desirable.

By studying the anatomy of the horse, you will find certain muscles of the back and loin that play a great part in the propulsion of the horse. With exercises you can supple and condition these muscles, preparing them for the actual feat of jumping. These muscles, due to their contraction and extension,

Backing is a good exercise in the long lines. At first, especially if your horse has an old problem associated with backing, you will no doubt meet with some resistance. Keeping the hands low, and using a slight give and take action, command the horse verbally to "back!" The moment he responds lighten the hand. Take note of Snipper's head, ears and mouth plus all over attitude of resistance.

are most important and will determine just how well your horse will be able to adjust his strides for proper takeoffs, stretch and extend the neck muscles, and in general have an overall supple and athletic appearance. By suppling exercises, you can build and condition these muscles so that when the time comes to jump your horse, he will be concentrating on the hurdle, not in devising ways to ease a sore and painful muscle. The work before a horse is jumped is extremely important and cannot be stressed enough, as he can only give his best when he has a clear stable mind, and a fit body.

One good suppling exercise is to walk your horse out at his normal speed, then urge him on to a faster walk. Keep urging him, but mind you keep him quiet and relaxed on a floating rein. Bring him back to his normal walk and then urge him on again. Eventually you will feel his shoulder and back muscles loosen and swing out in a reaching stride. In time he will be able to maintain this stride for long distances. It is also advisable to work him in circles, large and small, clockwise and counterclockwise. On these circles the body of the horse should gently curve from head to tail following the circle. These exercises supple a number of important lateral muscles.

These same exercises should be employed at the trot, and the canter. Both the normal and the extended trot; and also some on the semi-collected trot. However I do not stress too much collection on Quarter Horse jumpers.

Your horse at this point should be walking, trotting and cantering in circles, serpentines and loops. He should feel supple from head to tail, have developed balance and rhythm, be guiding almost imperceptibly. He should

Here, Snipper is giving to the bit and beginning to back passively in step with the trainer. Notice the relaxed attitude of his body, head, and neck as compared to all over resistance in previous photograph.

Moon's Comanche Gold, executing the normal trot with a degree of collection. He is being worked off the snaffle of the pelham bit. Quiet and relaxed he has good forward impulsion. These exercises are essential to developing suppleness, balance, and rhythm, plus obedience in your prospective hunter or jumper.

Comanche, being urged on to the extended trot on a loose rein. Notice position of head as compared with previous photograph where a degree of collection is evident. With more work his head will lower and his stride will lengthen to a greater degree.

Comanche, executes an extended canter on collection. Notice evidence of fluid forward impulsion and extension of stride. Head in a pleasing position of collection. You will notice Comanche is working on a light sensitive contact, yet ready for any command the trainer should give. The light, supple, well schooled horse should be able to exhibit extension of gait, and collection of gait at a walk, trot, and canter quietly, subtly and with the grace and eloquence of a dancer.

Working in serpentines helps supple the horse and helps teach him to go at an even pace during slight changes of direction. It also helps in responsiveness to the bit and to the aides.

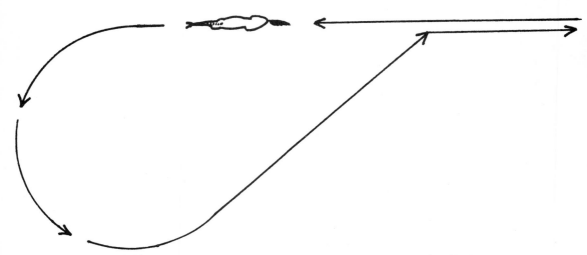

Large flat loops, as opposed to shoulder in or shoulder out movements, performed at the trot and canter both to the left and to the right are beneficial suppling exercises that help the horse with balance and rhythm.

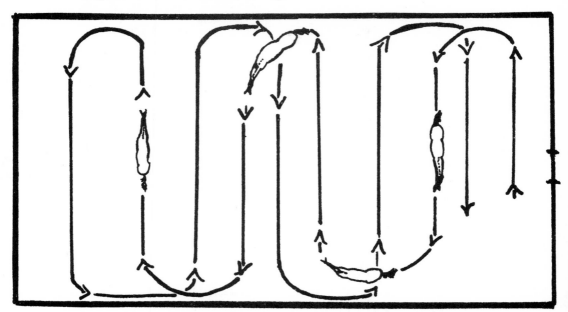

A series of serpentines back and forth across an arena or specific area is also a good suppling and balance exercise. It will also help your horse to come to the rein more readily than just straight line riding with no change of hand.

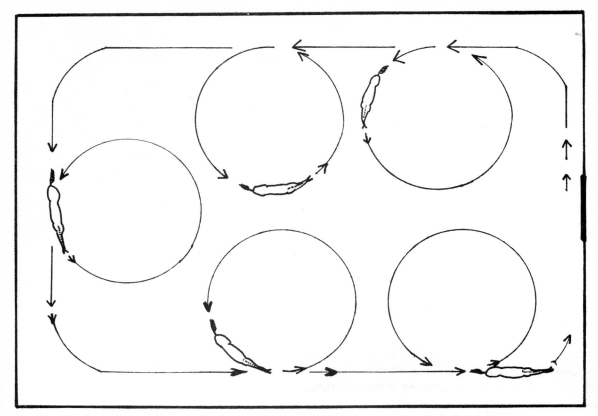

This is a very good exercise for your Quarter Horse. A series of circles performed at a trot first, and then after this has helped develop a stabilized gait, suppleness and rhythm, one can proceed at the canter. This exercise should be performed both ways of the ring or arena. This exercise also proves excellent for reining horses and pleasure horses under western tack as it will aid in the development of their balance and stabilization. The circles should be of a fairly large diameter at first, but with schooling they may be reduced in size until the reining horse is pivoting in the center. This exercise is also most desirable in your hunter or jumper as it will indeed make him a very handy horse. One must always remember that for successful work in collection of any degree, the work must be interspersed with periods of completely relaxed extension. When viewing many of the large Quarter Horse pleasure classes today, we find many horses performing that show evidence of never being given the opportunity to utilize their muscles and become really supple. They have been held at the same cadence for so many months—and yes, even years— that they would be totally unable to extend themselves at any of the gaits if asked. This is a sad situation, as the Quarter Horse is too fine an animal to become a "mechanical horse" with no brilliance!

be stable in his gaits and mental attitude, should easily and tactfully transcend from one phase to another through the stages of the walk, trot, canter and hand gallop.

Other excellent exercises are riding up and down hills, with halts, sliding down banks and general cross country riding.

Snipper Socks is being ridden up long rather steep hills. One must take great care in employing this exercise with a very young horse as it is very taxing. However your mature horse will benefit from this by building and conditioning muscles of propulsion. Here again you must take care even with mature horses, as these exercises are most strenuous. The horse should be taken slowly and not overdone, as holds true in any conditioning program. It will also help you in the way of developing a more secure seat over varied terrain. Care must be taken on the part of the rider so that he does not "hang" on his horse's mouth during the ascent of a steep slope.

Riding down hills is another very good exercise. A light steadying contact on the horse's rein is desirable. The rider should try to maintain position in the saddle and not interfere with the engaging hind quarters.

Occasional halts on the hill with the the horse's hind legs well under him is another good exercise in conditioning your future hunter or jumper.

Here Snipper Socks is stepping from one level to another while negotiating a steep hill. Maintain a secure seat in the saddle and a light contact on the rein. Keep your horse walking and never permit him to trot, canter or lunge—as some horses will try to do—up the hills. A steady even walk is the most desirable at this stage.

Starting down a fifty-foot-deep sand slide well balanced and light. A light contact on the reins to guide and steady the horse is desirable. Note open little and ring fingers of the rider. By closing these two fingers, the rider can steady the horse more securely or signal a change of direction. This shows a very soft yet effective contact. By employing and utilizing various exercises, and developing a sensitive responsive animal, a rider can truly enjoy his horse, whether he is ridden English or Western.

2

Work on the Longe Line

While you are riding and suppling your horse, but before he is ready to be ridden over fences, you may start introducing him to the actual function of jumping. Assuming he is longe line trained to walk, trot and canter, and reverse directions on command quietly and quickly, you may start work. Here again let me stress the quiet, stable approach to this new phase of training.

However it may be that your horse has never been schooled on a longe line, also referred to as a lunge line. Or perhaps he longes, but in one direction only; or he may have developed the bad habit of pulling on the longe.

Let us assume your Quarter Horse has never been trained to longe at all and that we must start at the very beginning. Here again, the ideal equipment is the longeing cavesson with its plated and hinged nose band, convenient rings and D's, and sturdy construction. Complete with its long web longe line it leaves little to be desired. If your tack room does not boast a longeing cavesson, a sturdy leather halter with round rings may be substituted. A rawhide bosal with *fiador* all properly adjusted is another satisfactory substitute for the longeing cavesson. Another piece of equipment is the longe line itself. This should not be less than twenty-five feet in length; and thirty-five feet of longe line is more desirable, as it will allow the trainer to always hold a reserve length of longe line in his hand.

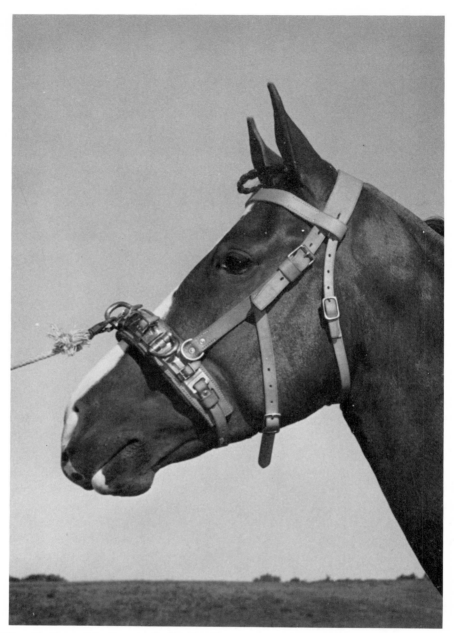

Jubilee Red, models the sturdy leather longe cavesson with the longe line attached. Notice the heavy plated nose band with three D rings. The D ring, on the lower cheek, is for the addition of a small strap to which a snaffle bit can be buckled and fitted to the horse for bitting. The nose band should be adjusted so as not to rest too low upon the horse's nose, nor too high so that it loses effectiveness; this will depend to a degree upon the individual animal. The jaw strap and nose band should be buckled just tight enough to prevent the cavesson from slipping out of position during schooling. Too tight a cavesson will only cause discomfort to the horse and defeat the purpose.

Assuming you are using the halter or hack-a-more in place of the longe cavesson, a length of cotton rope works quite well. A snap or lead chain may be attached to one end while a leather stop is worthwhile at the other end. If using the hack-a-more, you can tie the line directly to the bosal in the area of the heel knot. If using the halter you may snap the line into the halter ring; or if you prefer a lead chain, double it through the ring and snap it back into itself. This will work well if your horse is well mannered and leads well, responding to the halter quickly and lightly. If for some reason he does not respond to your satisfaction you may run the lead chain under his chin, through the round halter rings and snap it back into itself. I must caution you here to use discretion and tact, as this chain can be very severe when improperly used.

At this point an essential piece of equipment is the longe whip. This whip has a fairly long stock with a long lash that can be handled discreetly or snapped loudly at will.

Now that the horse is haltered, hack-a-mored — or the longe cavesson is in place with the longe line attached — you are ready to begin the first lesson in longeing.

Taking the coils of the longe line in the left hand, lead the horse out, walking beside him, using the right hand as the leading hand. You should attempt to longe him in a counterclockwise direction at first. Holding the longe line in the left hand and the whip in the right, keep the horse walking briskly; subtly drop back along his side encouraging him to walk ahead of you. At first he will no doubt insist on stopping and turning directly around to you. Stop him and start again. After several attempts and discreet persuasion with the whip and your voice, he should be describing a small circle around you. Your left hand should occasionally be playing out the longe line and acting in a leading manner, while your right hand is employed in handling the longe whip. Take it slow and easy. Repeat the command "walk" in a firm authoritative tone of voice to your horse to keep him walking at an even pace. He will perhaps begin to pull a little on the longe line as it is played out and the circles become larger. By short give-and-take pulls on the longe line, he will in time learn to work on the longe with a light pleasant contact — neither pulling, nor causing the longe line to slack and loop.

After your horse is walking calmly around you in this counterclockwise direction, and has completed a satisfactory training session, give the command "Whoa" or a short firm "ho!" At the same time exert a strong pull on the longe line. If your horse does not respond at once by stopping, repeat the command twice more. If he still pays no attention, repeat the command and at the same moment give a sharp short jerk on the longe line. If he turns and attempts to come towards you, snap the line and repeat "ho" again.

Jubilee Red exhibits a quiet relaxed walk on the longe line. Trainer's left hand is holding the coils of the longe line quite softly. Please notice forefinger and thumb manipulating extent of contact with the horse. Whip is acting in a trailing manner. Jubilee is between the trainer's two hands. Notice the trainer is moving on the circle with Jubilee.

Eventually through repetition of command and action, he will learn that the slight pull and verbal command of "ho" means immediate response is demanded.

When he is standing quietly and with no intention of moving, walk up to him and pet him to show him he has responded correctly.

The same method is employed to teach him to move in a clockwise direction, or to the right. Here you may expect a little more difficulty and no doubt there will be a need for more persistence on your part, as in the past your horse has most likely been handled a good deal more from the left than right side. It is a good idea to save this phase of training for the next day. I suggest you thoroughly school your horse to working the longe line in either direction, stopping and reversing on command at a walk before attempting to go on to the other gaits.

At the next lesson the horse should walk out on the longe, and knowing what is expected of him respond readily and willingly. After he has walked on the longe several minutes, give the command to stop and stand. At this point use the word "reverse," spoken in a firm tone of voice; at the same time indicate to the horse by action and whip that he is to move out to the right

Here take notice of the trainer's left hand. She has raised the forearm and hand. The longe line contact is still maintained by the forefinger and thumb; the trainer has stopped moving. By this slightly increased contact, Jubilee is shortening his circle quietly and tactfully, completely relaxed and at ease. Notice position of right foreleg as Jubilee begins to respond to the cue. Whip is still in the same position, as horse is still required to continue walking on the circle.

Moon's Comanche Gold, trotting on the longe. The trainer is moving with him and has just started to give the command to stop. Notice increased tension on the longe line, position of trainer's whip. When longeing, the trainer should strive to keep his hands low and in a comfortable working attitude.

at a walk. This is accomplished by picking up the longe line in the right hand and using the whip in the left hand. At the same time stepping to the left and continuing to repeat "reverse" and "walk" to the horse. Thus the animal, having already learned the command "walk," should respond, and after a few lessons of "ho," "reverse," and "walk" should be responding quickly. When this phase of the longe line training is firmly based in the horse's mind, we can begin to think of working him at a slow trot.

Working him a few minutes at the walk and repeating our already learned commands, we can now have him start to trot. Give the command "trot," at the same time shaking your whip. If no response is evident, give the command again and flick him lightly with the whip. This should induce him to

Comanche, standing quietly but at attention on the longe. Should your horse attempt to come towards you, repeat the command "ho" at the same time snapping the longe line at him, or you may shake the whip at him. If he attempts to move on the circle, repeat the command and persuade him to stop and stand until the command to move out is given. When rewarding your horse with a caress for obeying correctly, walk to the horse, pet him, and move back into position. Insist he stay in the same spot—with no dancing, creeping ahead or side stepping. This may take a good deal of patience on your part, but the horse of average intelligence should learn the procedure quite rapidly.

Comanche, trotting in a clockwise direction, or to the right on the longe. Here the trainer is walking on the circle. She has evidently just cracked the whip. Comanche continues to maintain a steady even trot. This is helping him to become stabilized in his gaits.

trot. Keep him trotting slowly. Watch him closely and when he even begins to think of walking, repeat the command "trot," and use the whip. Some horses become bored and lazy during the longe line schooling and must be kept attentive and on their toes. By constant work and repetition, your horse should be doing his longe line exercises smoothly and quietly.

By now you have begun to walk in a series of circles and in a straight line, with the horse describing circles around you at the desired gait. When he is slow trotting and trotting extended on the longe, reversing smoothly and quickly, you are ready to canter him. If his basic lessons have been faithfully

Madam Bellringer executes a reverse of direction at the trot. She was traveling in a clockwise direction, or to the right, at a trot. Given the command of "ho—reverse!" she has executed this movement without a moment's hesitation or interruption in rhythm. Notice position of trainer's arms. The looseness of the longe line indicates Bellringer is performing on command and subtle cue with no resistance. She is well on her way to mastering the techniques of the longe line.

carried out, he should make the transition into this phase with a minimum of effort. I must caution you that there are some horses who when first cantering on the longe line will take advantage of the situation to exhibit a display of high spirits and excessive speed. Of course these displays must immediately be dealt with and eliminated at once.

Perhaps at first you will run into some difficulty in the way of taking the correct lead. It could be that he will start off correctly but become dis-united. Or if he is an old horse with no real definite idea that there are two sides to him, you will have many trying moments. However trouble with leads on the longe usually occurs only in green colts or old spoiled horses. Colts adapt very rapidly to the longe line and one finds this training has been a real boon once the youngster is mounted.

When the horse has finished his longe line training, he should be able to stop, reverse and resume any commanded gait, including the canter or hand gallop, smoothly and very rapidly. He should be able to stop and stand smoothly and quietly from any gait. He should be able to stop, stand, and resume the same gait and direction on command.

Comanche executes an even-balanced canter on the longe. Here the trainer is using an across-the-body position with the whip. This is a difficult maneuver for the novice, for it may at times require the cracking of the whip backhanded, or other manipulations that may prove difficult and could lead to tangling of the longe lash, etc.

Comanche displays a rapid but smooth balanced reverse to the left from the canter. Notice the ears, legs and body position. Here the longe line is extremely loose, but the action is so rapid the trainer is unable to flip the slack even though she is stepping back and has already put her left hand and arm in the correct position. Notice the whip position with its long lash as the trainer accompanies the command with a crack of the whip. This will give you an idea of the speed at which this horse is working. Bear in mind all this was done on a light—even loose—contact with one verbal command!

Never underestimate the desirability of the longe line. More activities and exercises than can be imagined are possible as the result of correct longe line training techniques.

Here again Comanche executes a reverse at the canter, this time to the right. Again the action is very fast but smooth and in balance. Notice his ears and entire attitude. He shows he is working with balance and rhythm; he is calm and stable in his mental attitude. There is no fear or apprehension of the longe cavesson, the longe line, the longe whip or his trainer. He shows he is mentally and physically fit. The movements required of him are well within his capabilities.

3

An Introduction to Jumping

Now that your horse is thoroughly schooled in the longe line, it is time to introduce him to the standards, rails, and basic procedures and fundamentals of the act of jumping obstacles.

At first we start with no more than a pole or small log on the ground. Longe your horse over it at a walk and trot from either direction. It is also a good idea to set up two regular standards and longe the horse between them, from either direction. Some horses will have the tendency to "hurry" through, but if yours has had his basic lessons, he will on command relax and maintain a steady gait. When he is going through between the standards relaxed and steady, you are ready to lay a pole on the ground between the standards. Then proceed to work him over it at a walk and trot from either direction again. He is learning to look for an obstacle and is finding he has nothing to fear from it.

If you are working in a ring, place poles on the ground, and standards at various points around and on the ring. Then walking, with the horse describing his circles around you on the longe, at an even steady trot, let him go over and through the various obstacles. Take your time, do not overdo. Take plenty of time between obstacles; make sure the horse approaches the obstacles in a straight line and continues away in a straight line. Take care that he has freedom of his head and neck when negotiating the pole and

Madam Bellringer points her ears and maintaining a calm even trot proceeds between the standards. The first step in her introduction to the actual feat of jumping.

Still trotting calmly, the Madam willingly crosses the birch pole laid on the ground between the two training standards. You will notice by the position of her forelegs that she is giving a little hop over this obstacle. Head and neck are slightly lowered. Notice the trainer is maintaining a parallel position to the mare and is moving with her. Just enough contact through the longe line is being maintained to keep the Madam under control.

going between the standards. Maintain just enough contact to keep him under control. He will never become frightened of a fence if he has no unpleasant memories to associate with it.

By this method you have started to teach the horse that the fences are nothing to fear, that he may find one any place, and above all, that at this stage there is nothing to get excited about. Before long he will begin to point his ears and look for the next fence.

When you have your horse working well on the longe, lay a pole or small log on the ground, and mounted trot him over it from either direction. Do not just trot over the log, pull up, turn him around and trot back; but rather continue in a straight line, maintaining a steady calm trot.

After he has mastered this perfectly, with your added weight, place several

Jubilee Red approaching a series of eight permanent cavaletti. Notice the ears pointed forward surveying these new obstacles with inquiry and interest. Still he is maintaining a calm and even trot with no inclination to avoid the obstacle.

Head and neck lowered, looking ahead, Jubilee negotiates the cavaletti on a floating rein. Notice legs are not folded to as great a degree as is possible. Rider is maintaining a forward position in the saddle and not interfering with the horse's action. This is a good exercise to help you, as a rider, to perfect your balance and seat.

more poles on the ground. Now you ask, "where on the ground?" Trot your horse and measure his stride. Then place your poles so that he may comfortably trot over them in a straight line. Later by raising the cavaletti to a height of from six to eight inches from the ground, you will be teaching the horse to begin to fold his legs. These cavaletti exercises should be worked on a floating rein, with the rider maintaining a jumping position in the saddle. Negotiating the poles lowers the horse's head and neck and stabilizes his approach to the fence.

In time he will learn to use these logs, or cavaletti — combined with what he already knows about the extension of his gaits — to judge his takeoff point, and to adjust the length of his strides, which is most essential to a jumper when working a course.

Negotiating the cavaletti after some practice. Notice more prominent folding of the foreleg. Here Jubilee, is working the cavaletti on light contact. A picture of balance and rhythm. A horse working under pleasant conditions and enjoying his work is quite evident in this photograph.

Here again I stress: take it quiet and matter of fact with an even pace. Here again I caution you: don't over do! Never keep a horse working beyond his mental and physical span just because he is a willing subject. A horse that is physically fit and mentally alert usually, under pleasant and sensible training conditions, will find jumping a lark.

Now that your horse has mastered the cavaletti, he is ready to try his first real jump. However the cavaletti is a good exercise for not only the horse in training but a good exercise for the old seasoned campaigner as well.

You may construct a simple pole fence for your first attempt. Set up two low standards, use two cross poles not less than four inches in diameter. Rest one end of the cross poles on the standard pins and one end on the ground at the outside base of the opposite standard. It is a good idea to have one standard facing one way and the other the opposite so that the jump, when set up, can be used from either direction.

At the point where the poles cross in the middle of the jump, the top of the cross should be approximately eighteen inches from the ground. Now lay a pole on the ground from eighteen to twenty-four inches in front of the jump, and do likewise on the other side. This will not only give the horse a groundline, but will encourage him to stand back and fly his fences in good form. You should first show this jump to the horse, then take him back and start him on the longe. Work him at the same calm even trot. It is a good idea to longe him in several circles in the vicinity of the jump instead of

The cross pole fence is a simple but effective training fence. By placing one standard in one direction, and the other facing the opposite, you have a fence that can be jumped from either direction. The poles on the ground will not only give the fence a groundline, but will encourage your horse to stand back and fly his fences.

letting him jump it straight away after introduction to the fence. In this way he will not anticipate at just what moment he will be asked to negotiate the obstacle.

Set up several of these fences and work him over them. Be most careful to never repeat the same pattern continuously, as he will soon begin to anticipate the pattern. One purpose for crossing the poles is so that they will act as a guide for the horse, encouraging him to jump the fence straight in the middle. In competition, on tricky courses, and where time is an element, you may be jumping a fence off center or even at an angle; but for training purposes strive for the center of the fence.

Crossed poles are sometimes considered difficult, but I have had extremely good success with them when used in the manner I have described.

Madam Bellringer quietly inspects the training fence upon introduction to it. She finds there is nothing to fear, and nothing to become excited or upset about. Take plenty of time at this stage of training, let your horse inspect this new obstacle thoroughly.

The Madam negotiating the training fence from a trot for the very first time. Notice the extremely slow and uneven folding of the forelegs. Balancing on one hind leg, she is nearly ready to propel herself over the obstacle. She negotiates the fence willingly enough with no inclination to refuse, run out, change gait or exhibit any other undesirable actions. Here is where the previous training begins to pay off. Position of trainer is good. Left hand raised to clear the standard is in a leading position. Mare is between the trainer's two hands. The trainer will continue to move parallel to the mare so that she is able to continue away in a straight line, also to be in a position to correct any change in gait should the mare increase in speed on landing.

Another good fence at this stage of training is a low coop. This needs no pole on the ground, as by nature of its construction it has its own ground line, and a very slight spread — although it is not a spreading fence. It is a solid-appearing fence and most horses even after they have been properly introduced to it will need a little urging the first couple of times over it. Another excellent fence is the hedge or brush jump. If you do not have a hedge or brush box, you can simply construct a good brush jump with natural materials. At this point I would like to suggest that you construct a good

Madam Bellringer negotiating the cross poles from the opposite direction. As she has already been introduced to this fence once, it is not necssary to reintroduce her to it prior to change of direction. This is the first step in encouraging boldness in your jumper. Notice the slow and incomplete folding of the legs of this green horse. Notice the trainer is controlling the Madam by the forefinger and thumb of the left hand. She is not interfering with the mare's action, in any way, but is ready for instant correction should the need arise. Notice mare's left ear is ahead and she is taking the training fence in the center.

The low coop is a good training fence. It is a solid-appearing fence and the horse will no doubt need a bit of urging when you first attempt to put him over it. However, after the proper introduction and after negotiating it a couple of times you should have no problems.

number of different fences. When you show your Quarter Horse Hunter or Jumper, you may be using fences used by the regular hunter and jumper classes. A little paint and ingenuity go a long way in the construction of fences for the jumper course.

However, as progress is made in the jumping class of the American Quarter Horse Association, and in the Working Hunter class of the American Quarter Horse Association, more and better trained Quarter Horses will be competing, more and different fences — with better and more challenging courses —

The Madam buries her nose deep in the fragrant evergreen boughs in the hedge box, upon introduction to it. Here is an interesting obstacle and worth a look but again she finds it is nothing to fear. Always introduce your horse to the fence at the center. Always lead him straight up to it and never come at an angle; it is also a wise thing to back him a step or two, then turn him directly about and walk straight away from the fence.

First time over the hedge! A pole wing was added as a precaution, but it proved quite unnecessary. The Madam takes the fence in the center without breaking stride. A rewarding training session.

will become prevalent. Keep this in mind so that when the day comes, your Quarter Horse Jumper or Quarter Horse Working Hunter can meet and conquer the most challenging of fences and courses.

4

Jumping

As you continue with the schooling of your Quarter Horse, pause and make a short review of your own progress with your prospective jumper or hunter.

You have selected and outfitted your Quarter Horse in the proper forward seat jumping saddle with the wide tree. By now he should be working well in the hunting bridle with the large flat ring snaffle bit. He has been taken through a conditioning program in preparation for the actual feat of jumping. His gaits have been thoroughly stabilized. Subtle collection and extension have been exercised. His mental attitude is conditioned so that he approaches each new problem with a quiet stable outlook.

You have spent much time in the saddle learning to ride the correct forward seat. Wrists and fingers have become supple and pliable. You have practiced the art of following through during the extension of the horse's head and neck while negotiating the cavaletti, the series of poles or logs placed in line on the ground.

You have longed him over the low wide fences at the trot to develop his flight, while working at the trot has also strengthened his acrobatic ability.

If perhaps your horse has developed his action such that he can stride over a fence without knocking it down while working at the trot, raise the fence a few inches. This could mean anywhere from two to six inches depending upon the individual animal. You may also widen the ground poles to induce him to jump.

Now comes the time to let your Quarter Horse canter over the low schooling fences on the longe. If his training has been thorough and quiet, and if he is an apt pupil, the transition will be easy and natural.

I suggest you do not raise your fences for the first lessons, but then, after he has mastered the art of cantering over these low fences and continues to gallop away with no hesitation or "dwell," you may then, and only then, think about raising your fences. However, many horses, even after a good basic foundation, will have the tendency when first learning to canter or gallop over fences to, on landing, suddenly increase their speed. You must immediately and firmly bring the horse back to the desired pace. Insist he maintain the same even speed for a time. Then take him over the same fence in exactly the same manner as before.

A horse learns by repetition and experience. Always, in schooling, correct a fault at the fence at which it first occurs before attempting to present a new fence, hence a new problem, to the horse.

Another fence that may be introduced by now is the straight or vertical fence. The post and rail is an example of this type fence. This fence, having no actual ground line as has the coop, wall, etc., will present yet another problem for your horse to master.

When you first introduce him to the post and rail, it is a good idea to lay a pole on the ground approximately a foot or a foot and one-half in front of the fence as a guide and ground line. After your Quarter Horse has learned to jump this vertical fence with good form, to stand back and fly it well, the pole should be removed to simulate competitive fences of like construction.

Assuming that you have your Quarter Horse jumper performing on the longe at a trot and a canter over his fences, we will take a short look at some of the things that perhaps by now you have already noticed.

Perhaps you have noticed that sometimes your horse's hind legs tend to dangle down while he is in flight. He has not learned to fold his hind legs properly yet, but should in time. Another fault you may at one time or another encounter is over reaching. Your horse will take off too far back and is said to "reach for his fence." Of course this should with experience and schooling correct itself. Then again he may get in under his fence. This should also be corrected immediately. If your horse comes up to a fence and seems to hesitate, then leap over it at the last moment, measures must be immediately taken to correct this or he will shortly develop a pop over style of jumping that is most unpleasant as well as most undesirable.

If by chance you have a horse with the tendency to rush his fences in spite of a good basic foundation of stabilization of the gaits, there is a good corrective exercise. The moment the horse even begins to think of increasing his speed on the approach or anticipation of approach to a fence, circle him on the longe as many times as necessary to settle him. The same applies when schooling mounted. Only after he is completely settled and going quietly should you let him negotiate the obstacles. Keep him in the desired gait. This can be a most slow and trying process, but stick with it. Here again let me caution you, when the horse has made two or three, or yes, perhaps only one satisfactory jump, *quit!* Praise him and be done with jumping for the day.

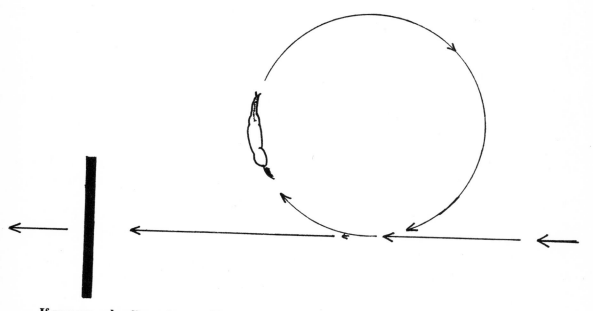

If you are schooling a horse with a desire to rush his fences, this simple exercise will aid in overcoming this fault. It may be applied either mounted or on the longe, depending on when the fault has occurred. The moment your horse starts to increase his speed, or even thinks of increasing it on approach—or even anticipation of approach—to a fence, circle him in a series of large circles until he is settled and going quietly. Patience is a prime requisite here.

When your horse exhibits a fault, you should consider what may have caused the fault to begin with. Possibly the horse is being pushed beyond his capabilities over fences of a height he is not mentally or physically able to cope with. His confidence in his trainer may not be secure, or perhaps he is not a particularly bold animal and has fear of a newly introduced fence. It could also be that his conformation is a hindrance to the art of jumping and to compensate he develops these habits or faults. Analyze the problem thoroughly and thereby find the cause, so that the cure may be affected.

Let us assume that your Quarter Horse Jumper or Hunter has progressed most satisfactorily and that you are thinking about jumping him over a fence mounted. Always bear in mind that before any violent activity, such as jumping, running, or reining, the horse should be slowly and thoroughly warmed and limbered up by walking, trotting and cantering.

After the horse is thoroughly warmed up, he should be ready to take you over the fence. At last you are beginning to reap the fruits of your labors. Your pulse quickens, your eye is keen, and you are ready for that first exhilarating leap over an obstacle aboard your faithful Quarter Horse.

It is a good practice to have the fences set at the same height that you have been using during the schooling sessions.

Remember that you must try to interfere as little as possible with your horse on approach, at point of takeoff, during flight itself and on landing. Keep in mind that you should maintain a continuous even contact with your horse and follow through with the extension of his head and neck. Be very careful not to violently raise the hands at the moment the horse lands and begins to gallop away, as this will cause a sharp painful jerk on his mouth. Another thing you must be certain to take into consideration is, that bumping your horse's back during any phase of the jump can be quite painful to the horse and may cause soreness in the kidney area. Which again will discourage even the most willing of jumpers.

Up until now you have been negotiating the cavaletti, practicing your position in the saddle and preparing yourself for the actual experience of taking your first real jump.

Starting at the same even trot that you have been working him at during the schooling sessions on the longe approach your first fence — sitting as quietly as possible on your horse. If you as a rider for any reason feel you are the least bit insecure, place your hand on the horse's neck. If your foundation training has been carefully and consistently carried out, your horse should carry you calmly over the fence and continue on his way quietly and at the same speed. However, if he does become upset, and breaks stride, quickly and firmly bring him back to the desired cadence. Maintain this speed until he is completely quiet and stable again. Remember, keep these training sessions calm and matter of fact. Do not hurry, and above all, never become angry and lose your head while schooling a horse. More harm can be done in five minutes' time than can be corrected in perhaps weeks.

Providing you have now mastered these low fences at the trot, and that you and your horse have been able to continue on over a series of fences set in a simple course, you are now ready to take the fences at a canter. Your horse has already learned to jump on the longe at the canter so there again the transition should be natural and easy.

After you have warmed and limbered your horse by his walking, trotting and cantering exercises you may take him over several fences at the trot. After this has been successfully accomplished, you may try the fences at a canter. Here again, if you feel the least bit insecure, place your hand on horse's neck. Use the same schooling fences and here again take it slowly.

Over these low fences there is no need for speed or increased forward impulsion, as the fences are well within the athletic ability of your horse, due to his previous conditioning and training. It is wise to work at these low fences until you have gained confidence and feel perfectly secure in the saddle during all phases of the jump itself. It should not be too long a time before you and your Quarter Horse jumper should be able to negotiate a simple course of fences in good form at an even cadenced pace.

At this point I would like to add a few words on riding a course. In competition it is usual to enter the ring and make a circle before sending your horse to the first fence. Let us assume you have done so and are now galloping towards the first obstacle. Your eyes should be to the fore, looking

When riding a course, whether it is in the confines of the show ring, or on the open outside hunt course, always look to the fore. Your eye should follow the course yet to be ridden. Always look ahead to the next fence. Here the rider is looking ahead, as is the horse. A light pleasing contact is being maintained. Notice the rein running between the ring and little finger of the rider's hand; this shows a light and sensitive feel of the horse's mouth. Horse and rider show a pleasant happy attitude, one of teamwork and compatibility.

over the fence and on along the course you are riding. Always look ahead to the next fence. Feel confident and secure; in other words "throw your heart over the fence and jump after it." I must caution you to never look down as a horse is going over a fence; never look back to see if you have scored a fault or gone clean. Concentrate on the fences and the course yet to be ridden. Always look ahead, never look back!

No doubt prior to now the temptation has been to raise the fences after a particularly good schooling session. Again patience and time are two very important factors. All fences should not be raised at the same time. Perhaps no more than one, depending upon your own individual animal.

After you have warmed your horse up, and taken him over the lower fences, you may introduce him to the raised fence. Walk him straight up to it, stop and let him smell it and look at it. Then take him back, make your circle and ride him at the fence. Do not be disappointed if he scores a knockdown, as he must still continue to learn the art of judging the various heights of different

The unpardonable sin of looking down!

Introduction to the raised post and rail fence. Jubilee Red tests the firmness of this top rail, which was raised three inches. Ears forward, eyes appraising, he will tuck this information away and be ready to utilize it when called upon to negotiate this fence. After introduction to the fence mounted, it is a wise thing to back your horse a few steps, then turning him directly about walk him away from the fence. By avoiding riding around the end of the fence and on to the next one, he will not be so inclined to get the idea that it is possible to run out and avoid jumping the fence.

types of fences, and to judge the necessary impulsion to raise and lift himself plus the rider's weight over the obstacle without touching it. This only comes with time and practice. You will find that many of the great jumping horses are older horses with years of experience and hundreds of fences behind them. At this time, your horse is still considered a very green jumper, or hunter.

Never raise a schooling fence more than three inches at the very most at any one time. This will depend again upon the individual horse. Usually, with most horses, more progress can be accomplished by raising the fence a mere inch at a time, although there are others who will do better if you raise it two or three inches. Always bear in mind: never go on to a greater height until your horse has mastered the first height. In this way you will be building up your horse's ability to jump heights, while at the same time maintaining his calm attitude.

Until now we have been working at only the slow gaits. Providing your horse has progressed satisfactorily up to the point where you are able to ride a simple course with a steady even pace, you may begin to think about galloping your horse a bit faster over his fences. You will no doubt score some knockdowns, he will probably make mistakes in his judgment or takeoff, etc.; but he should quickly learn to take the fences in stride at the new pace. After he has mastered this, and will gallop slowly or a bit faster over the course without becoming upset, a good exercise is to ride some fences slowly

Jubilee Red, landing after taking the first element of a double or in-and-out combination. Horse and rider looking ahead to the post and rail.

The one stride between fences. These combinations require the horse to be supple and obedient. Care must be taken that forward impulsion is not lost when negotiating a combination.

and others more rapidly. In this way you will have begun to school your horse for competition. In jumping competition we find various faces and combinations that require these changes in speed and stride. The working hunter negotiating a large outside course with long gallops between fences will be required to gallop on at a brisk hunting pace, showing his ability to stay with hounds. While in a handy hunter class the course may be such that it requires a somewhat slower pace, perhaps including a stop and dismount to lead over a fence.

For these changes in speed and stride you will find you have benefited from the extension and collection work and suppling exercises you have previously employed during the conditioning of your Quarter Horse. These same exercises, which you will faithfully continue, will keep your Quarter Horse in top physical condition.

Now that your horse has mastered the basic fundamentals of jumping, the fences can slowly be raised to competition heights.

Jumping out of the combination. This combination, or in-and-out, is commonly found in competition. It is found in the hunter classes as well as the jumper classes. By the addition of a third fence in the jumper classes it then becomes a treble. You may run into a little difficulty when first learning to ride and school over a combination. However, do not overdo; keep the training sessions calm and matter of fact. Bear in mind that you must maintain a good forward impulsion. Watch the length of stride of your horse in relation to the number of feet between the two fences. Twenty-four feet is a common distance between the two elements of the double.

Let me caution you that even though you are now ready to strive for height in your horse's performance, do not repeatedly ask him to leap fences of prodigious proportions. It is not only physically dangerous for the horse, but can be the deciding factor that prompts the animal, through physical discomfort and mental anguish, to develop undesirable and dangerous faults and habits.

Continue to concentrate on the quiet, stable and bold approach to obstacles of moderate height. A great variety of such fences — well within your horse's capabilities — will not upset your horse. It will teach him to go boldly on with no inclination to hesitate or refuse; it will eliminate the necessity of introducing your horse to each new obstacle he may encounter. This of course is very important as he will eventually be asked in competition to jump fences he is perhaps unfamiliar with.

Always remember that common sense plus good sound judgment, endless patience, and an open receptive mind are prerequisites of the successful horse trainer.

The Jumping Horse In Action

The following series of nine photographs show the mechanics of the jumping horse in action. In these photographs the animal is shown jumping freely with no impediment. Improper distribution of a rider's weight, or any other miscalculation of judgment on the part of the rider can produce a stiff or awkward jump.

By studying these photos, you will be able to see and understand the fluid changing of muscles, weight distribution, and the acrobatics performed by the jumping horse in action. You will come to realize the importance of a well conditioned, supple, fit body, and a stable, well adjusted mental approach to the problem. You will see the great power it requires to lift the horse over an obstacle. You will notice the great impact and shock that the forelegs are subjected to on landing. The tendons, and muscles, the horse's shock absorbers, must be in top physical condition to insure his physical well being in spite of these repeated strenuous activities.

A well conditioned, sensibly trained jumper will last for years. But, do not expect this to hold true if you do not have the patience to see your horse develop slowly and soundly. If you cannot wait to see your younger horse leaping great fences the horse will pay dearly. He may be brilliant this season, but what of three seasons later?

Madam Bellringer's hind quarters are moving forward in the completion of the last stride of approach to the fence before propelling herself over the obstacle. Take note of the rounded back and the fact that she is already beginning to make use of her head and neck. Notice the position of her left front ankle and leg as she prepares for the forehand to leave the ground.

The head and neck are extended forward and downward, while the hind legs propel the animal upwards and forwards. The slightly bent hock denotes that total forward and upward impulsion is not yet complete.

The mare is now in the first stage of flight. The hind legs shortly after propulsion are in the released spring stage. The hind legs have not as yet begun to fold. The mare's back is caving in, her head and neck are being stretched forward and downward.

By using her head and neck in a balancing action and bringing the weight forward, the mare will then be able to raise the hind quarters, enabling her to clear the obstacle. At this point the forelegs are unfolding in preparation for landing.

The moment before touchdown. The forelegs are extended, the head and neck are still extended but are starting to raise slightly. The hind quarters have now lifted over the obstacle.

The moment of landing. The head and neck are raised and stretching forward. The hindquarters are tucked up, the back is rounded. Notice the muscles and tendons of pasterns, forelegs, and chest, showing the distribution of weight. Also the impact and shock of landing. This will give you some idea of the strenuousness of jumping.

The hind legs have not touched down as yet. The head and neck have again extended forward and downward, enabling the mare to move forward in balance. The entire weight of the mare is supported by the left foreleg at this point. Notice the forward movement of the left hind leg.

The hind legs have landed and the right foreleg has finished extending and is now ready to begin a new stride. Head and neck still in a balancing attitude.

Continuing to gallop away in a straight line, the Madam strides out with no dwell or hesitation. Ready and willing to gallop on to the next obstacle. The completion of a satisfactory jump.

5

Working Hunters and Jumpers

When speaking of hunters and jumpers, it could be said that any hunter can jump, but not many jumpers can hunt. This perhaps sounds like an odd statement, so let us explore it farther.

A well schooled successful show jumper that can compete in open jumping, pussiance and other strictly jumping classes, may be wholly unsuited as a mount in the hunt field. Where as the jumper's primary function is to clear obstacles of great proportions, the working hunter must not only be able to have the ability to clear obstacles, although not so great in height as the jumper, but must do so with safety, good judgment, agreeability and explicit manners.

His gaits must be thoroughly stabilized with an even hunting pace; he should not air himself over fences, neither should he rub them. He should show he is capable of being ridden during the excitement of the hunt over rough and trappy country safely and comfortably. He should be serviceably sound: no lameness, broken wind or impairment of vision is allowed.

The Hunter judge scores the style and performance of the horse at each fence rather than just an accumulative number of faults incurred, as by the jumper negotiating the course. There is also a difference in the allowable fences in hunter and jumper classes. Hunter fences are to simulate those found in hunting country: gates, walls, logs, snake fences, rustic rails, aikens, a variety of coops, brush, etc. Jumper fences can be nearly any of these plus

Jubilee Red, working on the outside course. A hunter is presented with many problems when following hounds, or in the show ring. One of these is the ability to jump safely in rough country. Here Jubilee is jumping from one level to another. The severe drop on the takeoff side of this obstacle necessitates a jump of well over four feet, as the ground drops sharply away from the logs. On the landing side, the drop is approximately only three feet, six inches, with a slight uphill slope. Jubilee is negotiating the obstacle freely and safely. Notice the horse as well as the rider is looking ahead. A light pleasing contact on the rein presents an all-over picture of ease and comfort.

gaily painted panels, poles over barrels, triple bars, hog backs, double oxers, etc.

In hunter classes we find the outside course: a course laid out in a large open area, preferably a large grassy rolling field, where permanent jumps such as logs, coops, banks, rustics, water, living hedges, stone walls, etc. have been installed and are maintained. A hunter working the outside course gives the hunter judge a better opportunity to observe the horse under more normal hunting conditions than when the classes are held only in a show ring. Some hunters that are consistently shown in the show ring with a fair amount of success leave a great deal to be desired should they perform over a large, open,

Landing safely and comfortably on the drop side of this fence. The horse traveling at a brisk pace and jumping big will drop a considerable distance. On these type fences a horse's sound judgment is paramount.

well laid out outside course. There are also examples of the opposite where a hunter who performs passably well on the outside course will leave much to be desired when asked to perform in the enclosure of the show ring. Thus it is most desirable to acquaint and school your Quarter Horse for both the outside course, and the show ring or stadium course.

Most shows offering hunter classes are equipped to handle both classes and have the inside and outside courses available to their exhibitors.

When schooling your Quarter Horse as a working hunter, the basic methods employed in starting and schooling him are much the same as have been stated previously in this text. The emphasis should be placed on the quiet, stable approach: building and strengthening the horse's acrobatic and mental abilities; stressing style and manners; stabilization of gaits; and working at and achieving a harmony of relationship between the horse and rider at any given gait or activity.

The jumper must leap obstacles of height as well as width. Comanche negotiates the triple bar during a light training session on the longe line. Light schooling over fences between shows for the seasoned jumper is the most beneficial. It is unncessary and undesirable to ask him to repeatedly train over fences of the same magnitude as are found in competition.

The jumper in time becomes a finely trained individual. He is trained and conditioned to meet the challenges and demands of the shows and classes on the season's itinerary. He is brought up to a point that is comparable to the finely conditioned race horse.

After many competitions the jumper will anticipate the challenges of the difficult and exacting courses he is to be ridden over. Show day to the jumper is comparable to race day for the runner. Therefore, we have developed a sensitive responsive animal to the highest degree; and he of course responds accordingly.

When showing the working hunter, great care must be exercised so that even though the hunter is schooled and conditioned to his peak, express attention is given to keeping his style faultless, his manners above reproach, and to maintaining an even consistency of performance throughout the season. This continuity of consistency in all phases of the working hunter class is the only way that you can be assured of making your working hunter a champion.

6

Courses

The part the course designer plays in the success of a jumping competition is very important. Carefully planned courses with well constructed jumpable fences produce jumping of a high standard. These things are all necessary to the success of a show year after year. Exhibitors will return to these shows annually, where a show lacking good planning and management will in time dwindle and eventually become nonexistent. A show and its classes must appeal to the spectator as well as the exhibitor to be a continued annual success, looked forward to by spectators and exhibitors alike.

When planning a course, be it for jumpers or hunters, the course designer must first take into consideration the facilities at hand. The show ring, size, etc.; the outside course, if one is available; the materials on hand or that can be obtained for the construction of attractive fences and the general show ground layout.

Perhaps one of the most important tasks of the course designer is a thorough analysis of last year's classes and exhibitors: an analysis of the quality and standard of exhibitors who have in the past exhibited at this show, and of those that will perhaps be doing so in the future. Normally, exhibitors run the scale from the campaigning show string of the large and monied stable to the one horse amateur on a very limited budget. Even with the most intelligent planning not every class can be equally appropriate to each entry. However, it can be planned to be appropriate for the exhibitors as an overall group. Good planning and management is the thoughtful selection of various classes for the various categories of exhibitors. Care must be taken to not exclude the green, the novice, and the amateur horses and exhibitors. In this way, with courses planned accordingly, we can be assured of a successful and smooth-running show season after season.

It is a wise thing to schedule the easier classes early in the show with the more difficult and demanding classes later. This will give the exhibitor a reasonable opportunity to enter more than one class if so desired. Strenuous classes such as knockdown and outs, fault, and out and puissance — where the fences are very difficult, or the class may be subject to several jump offs — should be at the end of the show.

The course designer should pay special attention to the construction of the fences themselves. They should be attractive and jumpable. It is mandatory that he have a thorough working knowledge of the current rules and regulations governing the height, spreads, and other details of the fences and courses.

Placement of the fences is very important. Consideration of the footing, plus lay of the land so to speak, is also of great importance. Current weather conditions on show day must also be taken into consideration. Care must be exercised so that there are no fences or combinations that present an unfair advantage to any of the competitors, nor should they be so easy and unimaginative as to provide no challenge at all. Well laid out courses demand a well schooled and conditioned animal. Changes of direction, a chance to show his handiness — such as an ability to turn short, jump fences at an angle, going the shortest route in classes where time is an element, etc. — plus the ability of the rider to control the horse's gait smoothly are all challenges and demands of the well designed course.

The performances of the exhibitors over the actual courses will demonstrate just how well the course designer has performed his duty. By watching these performances much profit can be gleaned and later employed toward a steady improvement of the courses and the resulting higher quality of the exhibitor's performances.

In the 1966 rule book of the American Quarter Horse Association it specified the following rules in regard to the fences and courses for the Quarter Horse:

394. No horse shall be allowed to show in more than one approved AQHA registered jumping class per show.

395. Arena arrangements:

    a. Minimum of four jumps, Horses are to go twice around the course.

    b. Type of obstacles which may be used:

       1. Post & Rail (at least two)

    2. Chicken Coop.

    3. Stone Wall.

    4. Triple Bar.

  c. Obstacles should be located about 36 feet apart.

  d. Height of obstacles must be at least three feet. In case of ties, rails will be raised four inches on each go-round.

Let us take a closer look at this. Four fences, with approximately thirty-six feet between, comprise a very simple and elementary course that presents no real challenges for a jumper. More complete and challenging courses are needed for the advancement of the Quarter Horse as a jumper. This simple twice around the ring course can quickly degenerate into a dull and tiresome class with its whole purpose sadly defeated.

A simple course with at least one change of direction would be a step in the right direction. A change of direction and the addition of a combination would do much to further the advancement of the Quarter Horse as a jumper. Without these advancements in course design and fences, the Quarter Horse jumping classes will not advance but become stymied with an air of vapidity —

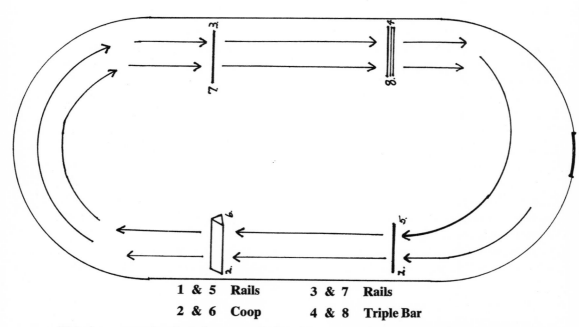

| 1 & 5 | Rails | 3 & 7 | Rails |
| 2 & 6 | Coop | 4 & 8 | Triple Bar |

This is a very simple twice around the ring course, it presents neither change of direction nor a combination. At present this is comparable to the American Quarter Horse Assocation jumper course requirements. More complete and more challenging courses are needed for the advancement of the American Quarter Horse as a jumper.

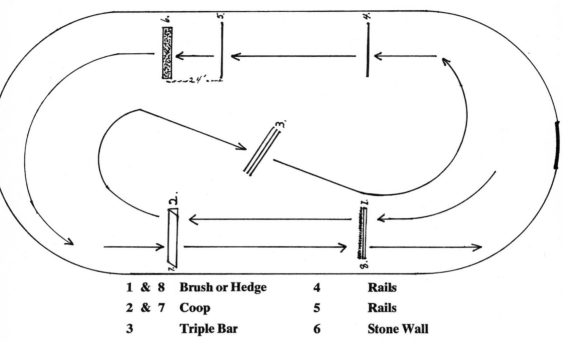

1 & 8	Brush or Hedge	4	Rails
2 & 7	Coop	5	Rails
3	Triple Bar	6	Stone Wall

This is a fairly simple course, but with the addition of a change of direction and the addition of an in-and-out, it presents more of a challenge than the twice around the ring course. It is a step in the right direction for betterment of Quarter Horse jumper courses.

with exhibitors and spectators alike going away with profound disappointment and dissatisfaction.

Let me stress again: there is a great need for better courses and a greater variety of fences for the Quarter Horse, for it is impossible for him to reach his full potential as a jumper if he is not given the opportunity to show what he is capable of doing over courses that are designed with this in mind. However, the arrangement and complexity of courses will depend to a certain extent upon the size of the arena or show ring in which the competition is to be held. A large roomy ring is of course the most desirable, but it is not always available. Despite this, a fair test of the exhibitors can be accomplished by a conscientious course designer.

In designing the course it is advisable to present the simpler fences early in the course, as this will help both the rider and the horse to be confident and go forward over these fences in preparation for the more difficult fences later in the course. A minimum of eight fences with perhaps as many as twelve in a

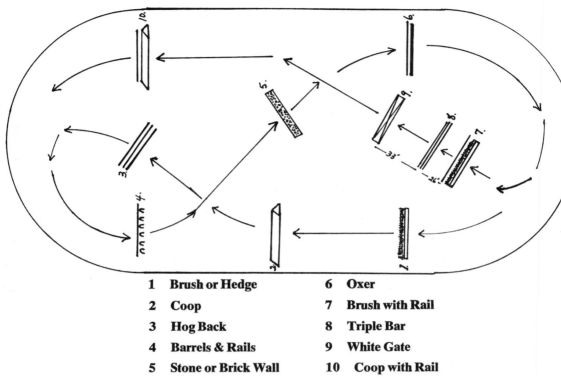

1	Brush or Hedge	6	Oxer
2	Coop	7	Brush with Rail
3	Hog Back	8	Triple Bar
4	Barrels & Rails	9	White Gate
5	Stone or Brick Wall	10	Coop with Rail

An open jumper course presenting problems in change of direction, a test of the horse's obedience and suppleness, and a test of his ability to jump spreads as well as heights. A good number of different obstacles making up the course also test his obedience and boldness. More courses of this caliber would do much to raise the standards of the American Quarter Horse as a Jumper.

course constitute courses of desirable length. This does not apply to puissance, where the fences are of such magnitude as to warrant a lesser number but of greater size.

Each fence should be a test of the horse. The combination will show his obedience and suppleness. The high fence of great proportions will show his ability to leap great heights, while jumps like the water jump will provide a test of his ability to leap broad obstacles.

A combination is a series of two and three fences set in line. A combination of two fences is called a double or in-and-out while a combination of three fences is called a treble.

The distance between the fences set in an in-and-out, or two fence combination, is usually twenty-three, twenty-four, or twenty-five feet and is considered as one stride. In trebles the distances can be set in one-stride distances be-

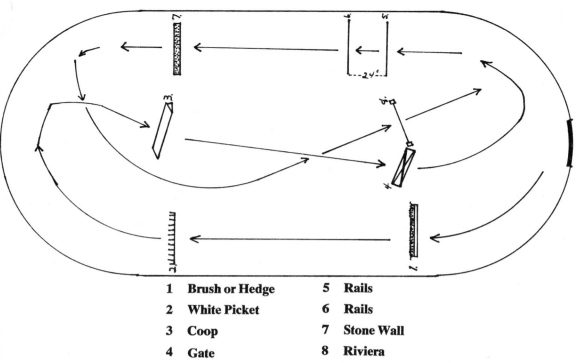

1	Brush or Hedge	5	Rails
2	White Picket	6	Rails
3	Coop	7	Stone Wall
4	Gate	8	Riviera

The working hunter course with fairly long gallops between fences to show an even hunting pace, his style over fences and his boldness over the various fences simulating those found in hunting country. This course is also designed to show his safety and manners.

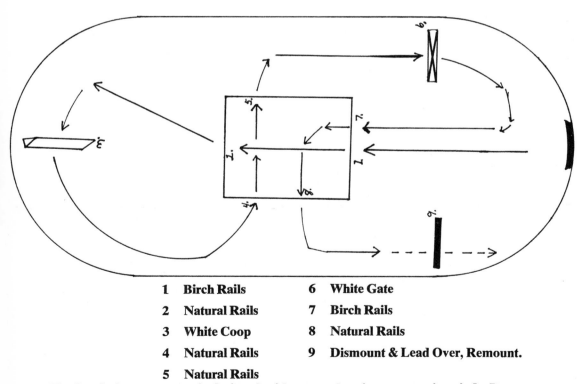

1	Birch Rails	6	White Gate
2	Natural Rails	7	Birch Rails
3	White Coop	8	Natural Rails
4	Natural Rails	9	Dismount & Lead Over, Remount.
5	Natural Rails		

The handy hunter course is designed with trappy hunting country in mind. It presents problems of change of direction within a limited number of feet, such as the inclusion of the pen jump, safety and style, and of course manners. By having the rider dismount and lead over a fence quietly without undue fuss and excitement, the judge will have gained a fair idea of the horse's manners when being handled from the ground as well as his obedience under pressure.

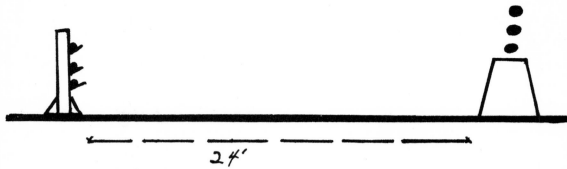

24'

A double or in-and-out. In this combination the horse jumps the first element, gallops one stride and jumps out. Usually twenty-three, twenty-four, or twenty-five feet are used between the elements. These different measurements indicate an increase or decrease in the length of stride to the exhibitor.

tween the elements, or a one-stride two-stride combination, or a two-stride one-stride combination. The distances of thirty-four, thirty-five or thirty-six feet are considered approximately two stride distances.

The distances are measured from the landing side of the first component to the takeoff side of the second component. The distance between the second fence, spread or vertical, is also measured from the landing side to the takeoff side of the third component.

The double and treble combination fences play an important part in the construction of good jumper courses. The in-and-out is a fence also commonly found in hunter classes. Both open and green classes. When designing courses for the hunters, bear in mind they must simulate a gallop after hounds in hunting country.

Where a well laid out outside field course is available, the course designer

24'   5'   33'

The treble. Here is a treble with a one stride, two stride combination. Note the five foot spread of the hog back or middle element. This is not measured as part of the twenty-four or thirty-three feet. Doubles and trebles are measured from the landing side of the first element to the takeoff side of the second element, and from the landing side of the second element to the takeoff side of the third and last element. When riding a combination and your horse refuses, you are required to jump the entire combination, not just the fence at which the fault occurred.

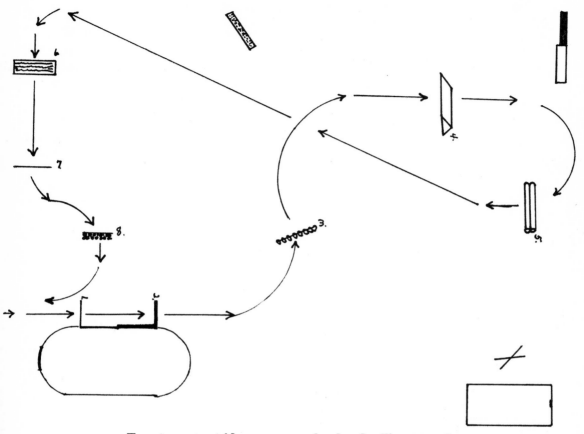

Twenty acre outside course over level and rolling ground.

1	Natural rails	5	Logs
2	Natural brush	6	Water
3	Tires	7	Rustic
4	Natural field coop	8	Piled tires

Over a large and roomy outside course such as this twenty acre one, the course will present problems such as jumping from one level to another, galloping at a brisk hunting pace up and down rolling hills, negotiating natural obstacles, and doing so with safety and manners. The Quarter Horse should really come to the fore in the working hunter class due to his calm even temperament and tractibility.

with a good knowledge of hunters and a lively imagination can design some interesting and challenging courses. It could be that due to the layout, it is possible to start the course inside the show ring, jump out, work on the outside course, and end up back in the show ring. This can produce some excellent courses.

I would like to suggest that the show management that has scheduled a Quarter Horse jumping class or a Quarter Horse working hunter class call on the services of a person who is familiar with and knowledgeable of course design. This suggestion is with an eye to the future; as yet the Quarter Horse courses are still very very limited.

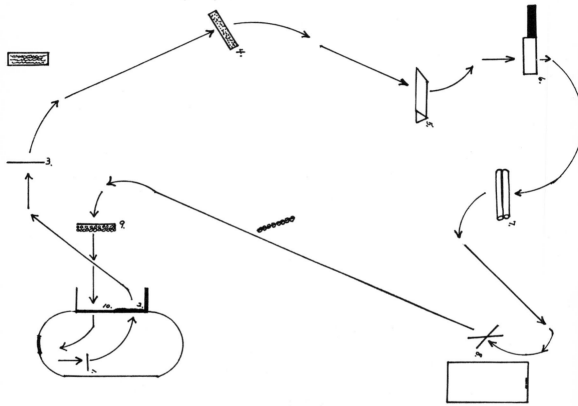

Twenty acre outside course over level and rolling ground, with course design beginning and ending in show ring.

1	White rails	6	Ditch
2	Living hedge	7	Logs
3	Rustic	8	Crossed logs
4	Field stone wall	9	Piled tires
5	Natural field coop	10	Stone wall with birch rail

Where a ring can be used in conjunction with the outside course, the course designer can create some interesting and challenging courses. Long brisk gallops on the outside course ending in the ring show the horse's hunting style as well as obedience, safety and manners.

Where facilities permit, the course designers can create some interesting and challenging courses by starting the course inside the show ring, jumping out, and returning to the show ring. Here Jubilee Red jumps the stone wall and rider on his way to the outside course. This fence is incorporated as a permanent part of the fence enclosing the ring.

Returning to the show ring after a successful round on the outside course. The well schooled hunter should finish the course with the same style and manners as exhibited at the beginning of the course. Here goes a well adjusted stable horse.

It is through interested members of the American Quarter Horse Association, and interested owners of the American Quarter Horse, that the Quarter Horse as a hunter and jumper will make marked progress and take his place in the horse world as a hunter and jumper, and be known for his proficiency as such, in addition to his already well known attributes in all phases of western events and racing.

7

Scoring the Quarter Horse Jumper and Working Hunter

The scoring of the Quarter Horse Jumper, and the Working Hunter, is not too different than the scoring of a jumper and hunter by the American Horse Shows Association. They both score on a fault basis with eliminations for approximately the same things.

Paragraph 392 of the American Quarter Horse Association, 1967 rule book states:

392. No horse shall be allowed to show in more than one approved AQHA registered jumping class per show. (This would not prevent a horse from being exhibited in both one approved Jumping class and one approved Working Hunter class.)

393. Arena arrangement:

a. There will be a minimum of four (4) obstacles; horses are to make a minimum of eight (8) jumps.

b. Type of obstacles which may be used:
   1. Post and Rail (at least two).
   2. Chicken coop.
   3. Stone Wall.
   4. Triple Bar.
   5. Brush Jump.

c. Obstacles should be located about 36 feet apart.

d. Height of obstacles must be at least three feet. In case of ties, rails will be raised four inches on each go-round.

394. Scoring:

a. Touch of obstacle with any portion of horse's body behind stifle: ½ fault.

b. Touch of obstacle with any portion of horse's body in front of stifle or with any part of rider or equipment: 1 fault.

c. Touch of standard or wing in jumping obstacle with any part of horse, rider, or equipment: 1 fault.

d. Knockdown of obstacle, standard, or wing with any portion of horse, rider, or equipment: 4 faults.

e. First disobedience (anywhere on course): 3 faults.

f. Second disobedience (anywhere on course): 6 faults.

g. Third disobedience (anywhere on course): Elimination.

h. Fall of horse and/or rider: Elimination.

i. Jumping obstacle before it is reset or without waiting for signal to proceed: Elimination.

j. Starting before starting signal; jumping obstacle before start whether forming part of course or not; jumping obstacle out of order; off course: Elimination.

k. Failure to enter ring within one minute of being called: Elimination.

l. Failure to cross the starting line within one minute after judge's signal to proceed: Elimination.

m. Jumping any obstacle before crossing starting line unless said obstacle is designated as a practice jump: Elimination.

n. At a brush element, the touch of the brush only, without touching the framework or pole on top thereof, is not scored as a fault.

395. Equipment:

a. Bridle: May be either double, Pelham, or plain snaffle. Chain curb may be used, but must be at least one-half inch in width, can not be twisted, must be the standard flat variety used with Pelham bit, and must meet the approval of the judge.

b. Breastplate: Optional.

c. Martingales: Optional.

d. Saddles: Flat saddles.

Working Hunter Class

396. No horse shall be allowed to show in more than one approved AQHA registered working hunter class per show. (This would not prevent a horse from being exhibited in both one approved Jumping class and one approved Working Hunter class.)

397. The Working Hunter class may be divided into two sections: Senior

Working Hunter and Junior Working Hunter, based on the age of the horse. In Junior Working Hunter, the same rules shall apply as in the all-ages or Senior Working Hunter, except that the minimum of obstacles should be three (3) feet.

398. A hunter course shall be any course which management deems a fair test of a hunter.

399. Arena arrangement:

a. Minimum of four obstacles to be jumped.

b. Types of obstacles which may be used:

1. Fences shall simulate obstacles found in the hunting field — such as post and rail, brush, stone wall, chicken coop, aiken, hedge, etc. A pole over brush, and jumps such as triple bar and hog backs are prohibited.

2. The top element of all fences must be securely placed so that a slight rub will not cause a knockdown.

3. Obstacles should be located at least fifty (50) feet apart; farther, if room permits.

4. Height of obstacles must be a minimum of three (3) feet and three (3) inches.

5. The use of wings on obstacles in hunter classes is recommended.

400. Scoring:

a. Performance: An even hunting pace, manners, and style of jumping, together with way of moving over the course as well as being jogged for soundness.

b. In all classes, judges shall line up horses on merit of performance before considering soundness. Horses may be required to show at a walk, trot, and canter.

c. Soundness: All horses must be serviceably sound. Any horse showing lameness, broken wind, or impairment of vision shall be refused an award.

401. Faults:

a. Light touches are not to be considered. Judges shall penalize unsafe jumping and bad form over fences, whether touched or untouched.

b. Faults for knockdowns, disobediences, and falls shall be the same as in the jumping class.

402. Equipment: Same as in jumping class.

If you are not a subscriber to the Quarter Horse Journal, breed publication of the American Quarter Horse Association, or you are not a member of the American Quarter Horse Association, you may write to the American Quarter Horse Association, P.O. Box 200, Amarillo, Texas 79105 and ask for their Official Handbook. They will be happy to mail you the booklet with the Corporation bylaws, registration rules and regulations, and the show and contest rules and regulations. Youth activities, also a very big item, are included in this handbook. The booklet is well worth adding to your reading material whether you own a registered Quarter Horse or not.

It is a wise thing to be completely familiar with the scoring systems used in the various hunter and jumper classes, whether they be Quarter Horse classes or open classes. A knowledge of these rules makes for a better understanding between the spectator and the exhibitor.

8

Fences

Throughout this book mention has been made of the various types of fences. No doubt there are those among you readers who have a very thorough knowledge of the individual jumps. There are also those among you who have ridden these fences many times. But I am sure there are those who would appreciate some clarification as to just what a coop, an oxer or a gate might be.

Let us first consider the standards. These are the two uprights on which the rails or fence itself shall rest. In American Horse Show Association approved shows, the standards are to be equipped with cups, preferably metal, that are attached to the inside of the standard so as to cause the rails to rest between the two standards at the desired height. This is an advantage, as it means the fence can be jumped from either direction — providing it is that type fence. It is also somewhat safer in competition than the ordinary pins. However for training purposes, the pin type standard is quite adequate.

It is preferable to have several sets of standards of different heights. This is especially convenient when schooling on the longe.

There are companies that manufacture these standards, fences and other jumping equipment. With a little planning, and a good hand with a square, saw and hammer, you can produce sturdy professional type standards and fences with only a fraction of the cost were you to purchase these ready made.

A couple of coats of gleaming white paint will complete the job and lend a show ring atmosphere to the training ring.

We will first deal with the post and rail type fence, as it is a common fence found in every course. It is considered a vertical fence by nature of its construction. Two standards support the rails, composing the fence. These rails should be spaced evenly, and enough rails should be used to make the fence appear more inviting and jumpable. Some horses have a tendency to become careless and lazy when presented with a flimsily constructed fence. A rail should be at least four inches in diameter and not less than twelve feet in length.

The largest percentage of rails are perhaps painted white, but rails of red and white, green and white, black and white, and other bright colors lend a more colorful and festive air to the show ring, in addition to making a larger variety of rail fences. Natural birch poles used as rails are desirable and lend the rustic touch of the open country to the affair. Here I must caution you: in some areas it is most difficult to find natural white birch poles that are perfectly straight. When using these always measure the height in the center of the fence as some poles with a slight bend, even though pegged at, say, four feet, may in the center be only three feet, nine inches. Always use your straightest rail on the top with the more crooked rails lower in the fence.

The snake fence is a type of rail fence set in a zigzag manner. Split rail fences are very popular. These have usually been treated with a wood preservative, which gives them a rich brown color. There are actually many types of post and rail fences, all jumpable and desirable.

The chicken coop or "coop" is a solid fence constructed on a modified "A" frame. The coop for the show ring is usually constructed in two sections to facilitate quick and easy handling by two men during the course of a horse show. The solid frame is covered with a thick plywood, and finally painted white. You will find coops of different heights and with corresponding widths.

The roll top coop is as the name implies: an approximate half circle giving the appearance of a half round. This is also of a solid construction.

The Toronto coop is, for an easy definition, half a roll top coop. The rounded portion is on the takeoff side. This is sometimes used in conjunction with rails.

In field or outside courses the coops are sometimes painted white, but a good many times they are left in the natural state. These coops are usually constructed in one piece of good one inch lumber. These field fences are exposed to hard use and the elements so they need to be of a more durable material than stadium jumps, which are at times stored under cover, or are used in an enclosed riding hall.

The wall is a jump that may be constructed in a modified "A" frame, or

The post and rail. The post and rail is a vertical or straight fence. This particular fence is constructed of birch rails. By the position of the standards it may be jumped from either direction.

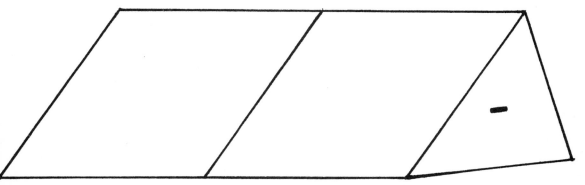

The chicken coop is a common fence found in competition. The stadium coop is usually constructed in two sections for ease of handling during the rush of a horse show.

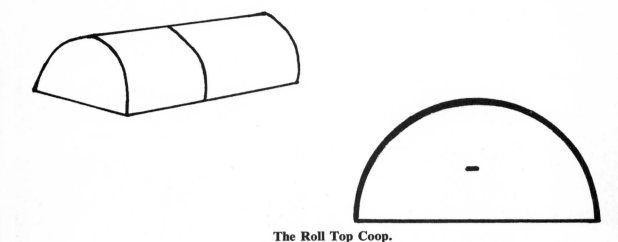

The Roll Top Coop.

simply as a straight sided fence. It can be constructed on skids, in one piece, or it can be a permanent wall of fieldstone or brick. A stadium wall is so constructed as to allow the addition of blocks of like material and color on top to raise the height in the event of jumpoffs or when using it in several different classes with different requirements as to height. Sometimes a wall is so constructed as to allow the addition of rails instead of blocks to raise the height. The wall constructed on skids is a heavy cumbersome affair and requires a tractor to haul it from one location to another.

A permanent fieldstone wall with a mortar cap incorporated into a field course is an addition to the course that is well worth the time and effort. Another very attractive wall is a red brick wall with its white mortar and white cap. Rails can be used to raise the height of these field fences if so desired.

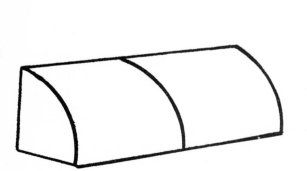

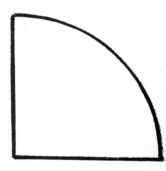

The Toronto Coop.

A sturdy field coop with rail or rider. By use of wooden brackets more rails may be added to raise the height of the fence for schooling or in competition.

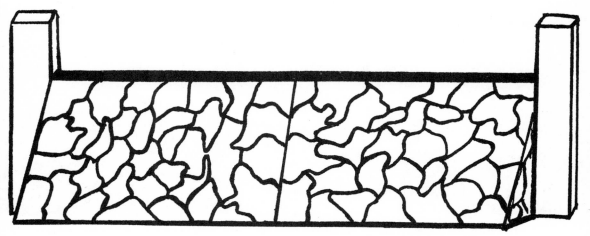

The Stone Wall. This wall is for show ring use. Built of heavy plywood in two sections this makes a very attractive jumpable fence. Blocks of like material and color may be added to raise the heights in the event of a jump off.

To build a hedge or brush jump the necessary elements are first a sturdy brush or hedge box. A good quantity of cut evergreens is most desirable, but if you do not have access to this type of growth any good brush, including sagebrush, can be utilized. A full thick brush box is the most desirable. If however you do not have a brush box, you can easily construct a wide and serviceable jump of cut brush piled neatly on the ground. Care must be taken that no sharp branches or twigs are so situated that in the event of misjudgment a horse might impale and injure himself on one of them. A rider or pole is many times placed above the brush jump.

Another hedge jump that is most beautiful as well as serviceable is the living hedge, trimmed and maintained throughout the year. Here you may incorporate it into a ring fence or locate it as a strip of living green at some point on the outside course. By trimming you can create sections of various heights

The hedge or brush jump. Evergreens produce a thick bushy hedge when the hedge box is adequatly stuffed. A rail or rider is many times used with this fence. This fence is pictured without a rider.

separated by ornate columns of living hedge. Although this fence takes time
to grow, and requires maintenance, it is extremely valuable in the schooling of
hunters, jumpers and three day event horses.

Ditches, banks, slides and water jumps are all worthwhile additions to any
establishments interested and involved in schooling hunters and jumpers. They
all present varied mental as well as athletic problems to the horse.

**The slide is a worthwhile addition to any training establishment. It may be that you
are fortunate enough to already have a natural slide at some point on your property.
This can be used in the design of courses as well as for training.**

The pen is a four sided one from which the horse jumps in and out again. It is usually of sufficient size to allow a change of direction after jumping the first element, or into the pen. This is left to the discretion of the course designer or the trainer. The pen is very popular with handy hunter classes and the horse is frequently asked to jump into the pen, make a right angle turn and jump out.

A pile of logs is a field or outside course fence that will last for years. If natural logs are not available, used utility poles can perhaps be obtained and will do very nicely. If securing these logs is a problem, less logs can be used if you build the log jump in a pyramid shape, instead of a solid pile of logs. When these fences are to be used by green horses, pony hunters, and made jumpers and hunters, a lighter log serving as the top log is handy as it may be removed or added, depending upon the horses that are being schooled that particular day.

Old discarded tires make another excellent fence. The tires are strung on a

The permanent log fence on the outside course will last for years.

This four foot high pile of discarded tires, approximately six feet wide, is a big solid appearing fence for the outside course. The horse that is mentally as well as physically fit and stable will approach and negotiate a large fence with the same ease and grace as he exhibits at a smaller one.

log and set on two end posts. They are very heavy and you will need some help in placing them on the posts after the tires are strung on the log. If for some reason you do not wish to construct this as a permanent fence, a pile of tires can be used, although they are a bit dangerous as a horse may become entangled in them and it could result in a very nasty accident.

Any field or outside course fence should not be less than twenty feet wide. Twenty foot panels are at times set in pasture fences to allow the local hunt enthusiasts to ride across this land after the hunt or when just out for a pleasure hack. If you live in an area where there is a hunt club and would like to ride your Quarter Horse across some of this land it is advisable to check first with the Master and obtain permission.

In jumper classes we find a number of spread fences that demand a horse jump great widths combined with heights. Some of these are the hog back, triple bar, oxer and double oxer, and parallel bars. The American Horse Show

Association rules have specific specifications as to the minimum spreads and heights of these fences. The rules are pertinent to the class such as green jumper, regular, puissance, etc. In the near future it will become mandatory for the American Quarter Horse Association to standardize the minimums and maximums of spreads in relation to the heights of the fences. For as it stands now, with no required minimum or maximum of widths, the decision is left entirely up to the individual show committee, or course designer. This could result in one class in one show using the American Horse Show Association standards for minimums and maximums for width of spread fences, while another class at another show could be set up by the "guess and by gosh" method. Only through the efforts of hard working interested people in the American Quarter Horse Association can these problems and deficiencies be eliminated.

The hog back is a three element fence composed so that the two outside elements are of the same height with the middle element up to the required height. The two outside elements are placed to fit the standard of minimum or maximum spread.

The triple bar is a fence of three rails graduating in height from say two feet, six inches to three feet, six inches to four feet, six inches — with perhaps a five foot spread. It is advisable to allow at least a nine inch difference in the heights of the various elements of the spread jump. This will help eliminate the error of having the first element too high in relation to the highest element.

The oxer may be constructed with brush and rails, or a coop and rails, hay

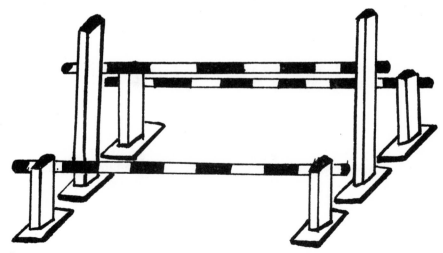

The hog back is a three element fence making it a spread type fence. This fence will test the horse's ability to jump great widths as well as heights.

The Triple Bar is a spread type jumper fence. It is high as well as wide.

bales and rails and other satisfactory fences set together. These two-element fences are of different heights and can be set to facilitate a spread.

Parallel bars can be described as two post and rail fences set perhaps five feet apart and both the same height. The space between may be filled with brush or some other suitable material to make it appear more solid and inviting. This is considered quite a difficult fence.

A panel fence is a large solid panel usually painted white with gay and colorful designs painted on it. Bullseyes or targets, stars, and the like are quite common. They are usually constructed of a large plywood panel attached to a rail for easy hanging in the brackets or from the pins. Here one's imagination in the way of design can run rampant.

The detour or road barricade is usually made of a two-by-twelve plank with black and white or yellow and white stripes, set at a diagonal, painted on it —

The Oxer. This Oxer is constructed with the brush and a rail. This is also a spread type fence.

Parallel Bars are usually constructed of post and rails of the same height with a spread of perhaps four to five feet between the two elements. It is advisable to fill the space between the two with brush, hay bales or some other suitable material.

The Panel. Here one's imagination can run rampant in the way of design and color. It is usually used in conjunction with rails.

much like those you see along the roadway of an afternoon's drive along a section of highway where construction is in progress.

Barrels with rails over them are another type of popular jumper fence. The barrels are fifty gallon metal drums painted white or in one gay color, or in a combination of colors. These of course are used in conjunction with the rails

The Barricade or Detour Sign. These can be yellow and black as well as white and black. One must take great care in the use of yellow paint as it does have a tendency to blend with the crowds when they are on the same level as the course.

to obtain the desired height. If you happen to live in a dairy country or can obtain used or discarded ten gallon milk cans, painted white, used with poles they make a fine training fence or one small enough to use with pony hunters and jumpers. In the horse's eye they are the same as the fifty gallon barrels and poles, only of a smaller dimension. As a result of this introduction to the smaller cans, the introduction of the larger barrels and poles comes quite naturally to the horse.

The white picket simulates a picket fence, similar to one you might find enclosing a lawn or yard. One-by-fours are fastened securely to a top rail, a two-by-four works very nicely, with a two-by-four for reinforcement and to hold the bottom of the pickets in place. The height of the picket can be a matter of preference for training. A four foot picket is desirable for competition.

The white gate is constructed of good solid lumber just as a good farm gate

Comanche negotiates a fence constructed of discarded ten gallon milk cans and rails. This is a good training fence as the transition to rails and fifty gallon drums is quite simple.

The white picket. This is found in both hunter and jumper classes.

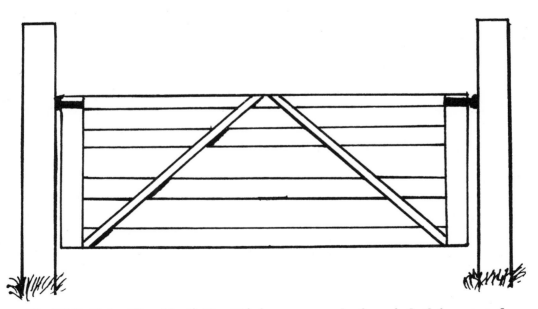

The White Gate. The old reliable. This is a very popular fence in both jumper and hunter classes.

The Riviera. This is actually a form of gate, sometimes found in use as a garden gate on expansive estates. It is graceful in design and adds to any course.

is made. It should look as though it is sturdy enough and of a sufficient height so that if taken out of the show ring and hung on a gate post, it would close the opening and hold horses or cattle in a farm yard or pasture.

The Riviera is a fence that is sometimes constructed similarly to the picket fence, but instead of being straight across the top as is the picket, it has been cut in a gentle downward curve and up again so that the two outsides are high and the lowest point of the curve is at the middle point of the fence.

This will help to give you an idea of the large number of fences that are to be found in competition today. By attending a large hunter and jumper show, and observing the fences and the course designs, you will be adding to your knowledge of what to expect, what to work for, and what your ultimate goal should be.

It will also serve you well to take the time and effort to visit some of the prominent and successful stables of hunters and jumpers and observe some of the training sessions. I am sure it is an experience you will not only enjoy but profit from as well. You will perhaps be fortunate enough to observe not only the good and helpful but the evils and pitfalls to avoid.

Let us go on, and by promotion, training and competitions worthy of the American Quarter Horse, let his name become synonymous with jumper!

9

Short History Of Jumping

Perhaps there are those among you who would like to know just what started the sport of leaping horses over obstacles. It could best be said that it was the result of a sport which originally led to the jumping of horses.

History tells us that in England the agriculture areas of that country were run with large open commons where cattle were raised, straying at will on the vast open cornfields much as cattle on open range land do today here in America.

In the fourteenth century the first movements of enclosure became evident. It came about as a result of the disturbance of the labor market and relationship of laborers to their employers. It was not until the eighteenth and nineteenth centuries that the Enclosure Movement came to the fore. This movement, where the open fields were fenced and village communities were transferred to a landlord with tenant farmers and hired laborers helped to bring about what we know today as our competitive jumping contests.

After the enclosures were authorized by acts of Parliament the movement became quite rapid. More than six million acres were enclosed in a comparatively short time.

Up until this time a gentleman could ride cross country with the most formidable obstacle a small ditch, stream, or bank at best. However after the Enclosure Act, fields and pastures were fenced with hawthorn hedge rows, stone walls, and some stake and binders and some post and rails. To continue hunting on horseback, the gentleman needed a mount that could leap these obstacles and continue on to follow the hunt. Of course the main object was to leap the fence with no thought or knowledge of our modern day forward seat, which is actually only a little more than seventy-five years old. So the prime object was for the horse to leap the fence and continue on his way.

It was during the time of eighteenth-century England, in the Stuart era, that horses from Arabia and Barbary were imported as sires for their race horses and hunters. In the reign of George III, the English horses were considered some of the finest in the world, whether race horse, hunter or draft horse.

The first mention I have found of a jumping competition, as such, was at a Harness Show in Paris, France in the year 1866. At this exhibition the competitors were sent out to jump some natural obstacles in the nearby countryside. As can well be imagined, this held little or no spectator interest. At a later date a few simple fences were constructed on the show grounds. This was somewhat better received by the spectators and exhibitors as well. The fences were very simple and the rules were left in the hands of the judge. As yet there had been no standardization of rules at all.

In 1876, or approximately ten years later, there is mention of a class of arena jumping at a show in London, England. The competitions were called "lepping" or leaping contests. Once established, horse show jumping made comparatively swift progress.

The first international jumping competition took place in London, England, in the year 1907.

In the year 1912 jumping was first included in the fifth modern Olympic Games, held at Stockholm, Sweden. Seven nations competed in the equestrian events at this Olympiad. Lieutenant A. Nordlander, of Sweden, was the individual winner, with Sweden also capturing the unofficial team title.

The first recorded equestrian event of the Olympic games dates back to the twenty-fifth Olympics in the year 680 B.C. This was a four-horse chariot race. The first recorded mounted horse race was in 648 B.C. at the thirty-third Olympiad.

Pagondas, a Theban, was the first winner whose name has stood the test of time and been recorded in the annals of equine history. He drove his chariot teams to victory time and time again.

Ireland is credited with being the cradle of the steeplechase. This can be traced back to the year 1752. There is a record of a four and one-half mile race cross country from the Church of Buttevant to the steeple of St. Leger. The record tells us that Mr. O'Callaghan and Mr. Edmund Blake were the participants. At the very early steeplechases, in addition to the money, the prize was perhaps a hogshead of claret, a cask of rum and a pipe or port. Here it is evident jumping and hunting horses were used in the hunt a good many years before any actual show ring competition was engaged in.

Competitive jumping such as we are familiar with today is indeed a far cry from that first exhibition of "lepping" horses in the France of 1866.

These are only a very few facts in the history of show jumping. Perhaps it will have been of interest to you, and have helped to give you an idea of how this challenging and exciting sport came to be.

Wherever there are horses and horsemen, there is an inevitable leaning toward the wager. The Quarter Horse is well aware of this. In days gone by he stood, the center of attention on some dusty street, while owner after owner pitted their swiftest steeds against his flying hooves in the quarter mile sprint. Thus earning him the name of Quarter Horse. But now the time has come for him to invade the show ring of the jumper and still to win the wager for his owner and for his many admirers!

10

Conclusion

The American Quarter Horse has indeed come a long way from his humble beginnings in a new and wild country. In the 1600's he was known as the Colonial Quarter of a Mile Running Horse. Today he is known simply as a Quarter Horse. His list of accomplishments is long, and it seems to grow longer with every passing year.

The Quarter Horse of early America: He found favor with General George Washington as a sprinter on those narrow dusty streets of frontier America. He found his way west across the vast stretches of plains and over the rugged mountain passes looking through the collar of a harness. He plowed the fields, and carried the kids to school. He pulled the family buggy to church on Sunday. He herded cattle in the heat of the day and trailed the herds from Texas to Montana. He hauled great freight wagon loads of goods so that remote frontier towns could survive and prosper. Yes, wherever a horse was needed to do the job and do it well, the Quarter Horse was there.

The Quarter Horse, the horse with a heart as big as all outdoors. The horse that could work six days a week and race on Sunday. The horse that could do it all and more when asked.

Disposition, versatility and adaptability are synonymous with Quarter Horses.

Now, supporters and admirers of the American Quarter Horse can see him continue to stride forward in this new venture and add still another facet to his already lengthy list of achievements.

When training the noble Quarter Horse, be it for the many phases of Western activities, or for this new venture into the world of the Hunter and Jumper, respect and preserve his personality. Develop a bond of respect and understanding between thee and he. Strive for and achieve a harmony of relationship so that as a team you are as one.

Progress together, and the future is yours!

Index